RABBIT HOLES

Naiche Lizzette Parker

Cover Design: Feri84
Interior Artwork: Vladislav Andonov
Publisher: Crooked Queen Literature
ISBN: 978-1545395899

1. Poetry 2. Magical Realism 3. Anthology 4. Fiction
First Edition

For the lambs who are also wolves.

Dear Reader,

Rabbit holes. What does yours look like? Do yellow eyes stare back at you from the dark? Do wildflowers grow? Is it born from your imagination? Heartbreak? Fear? What does it take for you to become Alice? Do you choose to fall?

The foreword to my first anthology, Paper and Bones, is riddled with ramblings. It is a web of dreams and aesthetics and wants, all the fairy dust wrung out from my hair sprinkled onto its page. For that is what Paper and Bones was. A tribute to the gorgeous chaos I've always known. My girlhood. My magic.

Rabbit Holes owns no foreword. These hands are for climbing out and crawling in. There was that. And now there is this.

It is not a fairytale. It is a becoming.

Sincerely,
NLP

SKIN

i have been the girl in the red dress,
red dress on the floor
next to her pride, makeup running.

i have been the pedestal and
the marble on it.

i have been the glass half full,
half empty,
half broken – thrown at
the wall.

i have been the bullet,
i have been the wound,
i have been everything that it took
to become neither.

i have always wanted the road.
i have been a tire-marked soul.

i have picked the roses
that stem from my chest,
given them away,
then blamed them for dying.

i have been the sinner,
the saint,
no religion,
every religion,
godless, god herself.

i have been so much of him,

of her,
that i became the mask of me.

i have been the bluebird,
i have been blue.

i have been the scars, the ink, the birthmarks,
broken bones, lightening cuts,
bruises, smoke, hair dye, and lipstick.

change the paint on the walls;
i am still home.

UNTITLED

i saw you again,
and the songs on the radio
didn't prepare me for it.

when we hugged, your arms felt less like home
and more like the strange and terrifying fondness
of the motel super 8's we used to stay in
when the car would break down.

i was afraid of you.

of time,
of how it doesn't heal at all,
of how frail the years seemed
in your chokehold.

i had a point to prove,
that you had changed
or hadn't at all?
that i had, maybe.

i remembered why i fell for you,
and that was the worst part of it.
there you were, a haunted house.
there i was, so good at crawling into bed
with old ghosts.

HOMECOMING

revisiting my childhood home is a clenched fist.

in the hands of its second family,
all the flowers we planted that summer have died.
call it metaphorical.

when their walls howl,
when their floors creak,
i wonder if my parents' screams are still echoing.
i wonder if there is a universe where we are still sitting
down to dinner.

when they think they are being haunted by ghosts,
i wonder if they are right.

i pay my respects to
this cemetery of all the mothers fathers children
we tried to be,
of all the selves we wore
that never fit.

the shutters look like the eyes
on a face
i've forgotten the name of.

we drive away from the doorframe
on which i once carved
"forever."

BECOMING

my hands are full
with all the poetry i cannot write.

i am molten;
i am decaying.

i weep at the grave
of the girl i was before the pen.

there is nothing romantic
about my mind.
i dress my words in pink
and shout the names of my lovers
until they rhyme.

i am paper,
i am endless,
what a curse,
to never die.

but everyone wants to love a writer.

like blood and ink,
they always want you until you stain.

OVER BEFORE IT STARTED

first date ideas:
the museum close to closing,
just some dead light and our hearts on the floor,
getting to know you through the eyes of what
you're looking at,
all the things that haunt you back.
breathing life into brushstrokes
and canvas ghosts,
so with you and so alone.

mid-july tuxedos and ball gowns,
going to a decaying field
with a boombox and the one from the
coffee shop to resuscitate it,
strawberry juice dribbling down your chin and "no
leave it,"
with every chuckle and dip barefoot
to cash and presley on repeat.

bookshop hopping and leaving
love letters in every stephen king
because "neruda don't need 'em,"
catching your eye between stacks
and showing you the line of the book
that broke my heart,
a kind of
warning,
a kind of
begging.

a cardboard box and sharpie:

TIME MACHINE,
we sit inside of it and roll our eyes,
knees touching, and play a game of memories
that don't count until the ice breaks by mistake
and suddenly my dad is in there with us,
your uncle's hand,
the night of the storm,
the day your fear of abandonment was born
shared by that of the scars on my back.
it's already too late for us when
you whisper, "it worked."

or, i guess,
we can start at the end,
on the street,
all your clothes on the pavement,
laughing
and yelling about how you cheated on me
just to cause a scene.
drunk and buckling over after,
and you look at me like, "that was hilarious"
when a bright young thing just passing by
catches your eye
for a millisecond too long.

the next three years shake
with my laughter
when i agree.

IF HE WANTS TO LIVE FOREVER, LET HIM DO IT ON HIS OWN

when the boy breaks you,
rip him like paper.
evict him from the stanzas,
drain the pen of ink,
and bleed him to the bone.

do not immortalize him
or keep him warm inside
the cottage of your poetry.
no milk and cookies,
no words on stone.

when the boy breaks you,
eat him whole
with the teeth of your silence
and the tongue of your apathy.

"you deserve better."
i do.
"will you write about me?"
i won't.

I AM

i sit down to dinner with every girl i have been,
every woman i will be.
a feast of white bread and red wine
spilling from the tables into our eager palms,
a reconciliation.

all the same brown eyes,
all in dresses like the feathers on ravens,
like the color of bone.

at the children's table,
five asks eight if mom and dad are going to make it.
sixteen and i weep.

seventeen's bones prod her skin
when she says she's not hungry,
and thirty holds her like a mother would a child,
belly full.

ten twines my hair in braids, then scowls
when twenty-five unravels them.
on me, thirteen's birthmarks have become bruises,
red scars lightening white,
handprints the color of ghosts.

around the table, aging up,
we whisper the names of people
who have promised us forever.
around the table, aging down, we whisper,
gone, gone, gone.

i fold myself into tight embraces,

eighty yelling that it is beautiful where she is,
and my hands ache for her like a mountain climb.

twelve asks if we're going to be okay;
i tell the truth or lie when i say
that we're just fine.

there are nights i mourn them more
than i can celebrate myself.
there are nights they seem farther away from me
than i can reach,
clinging onto snakeskin
like a winter coat.

but too long are the lengths
i have gone to earn these bones
to give up now.

for i am a wildfire.
my sole purpose is to grow.

GIRLHOOD

it was the summer we were all ready to die.
it was the summer we were terrified to go outside.
with their masks on,
with our blood ready,

it was the summer of scream:
don't go out after dark,
don't make eye contact,
don't take your jacket off.

ready?
begin.

it was the summer my bare midriff
became a mating call.

this morning,
i passed through a line of construction workers,
wading through the shark's den
like my body had some debt to pay
for being.

the slits of their eyes,
the token of my flesh.

i am not new to this race
to be the final girl,
turning on my sisters
just to stomach a turn with him.

the horror movie madonna,

soul stolen
then dangled over my head as a prize.

it was the summer we became so sad,
it was the summer the princes decided
to catcall us back to life.

break the spell,
come on baby,
smile.

it was the summer we gave up our hearts
in the black market of girlhood,
traded them in for hotter blood
and thicker skin.

parts of our bodies that had not yet
been touched with permission
fondled in the hallway,
smiling goodbye to dignity,
shed like petals off snatched flowers.

it was the summer i learned
how to survive despite him,
and he just learned
how to survive.

but i must have played this game well;
final scene,
blood on my face,
wearing white,
for in our high school yearbook

i was voted most likely to be a runaway bride.

(god, i hope so.)

now hand me the knife.

GRIMM'S GIRLS

grimm's girls sleep dead deep in the forest,
screech like the blackbirds that live in their chests.

grimm's girls are made of wicker and soot and elm,
are fairytales, are ivory, are hell.

grimm's girls leave breadcrumbs
that look like bones,

baskets filled with stale cookies and rotten apples,
sink their fingernails into the earth like coming home.

grimm's girls are the witches
with long noses and emerald eyes,
teeth bared like the shards of a broken mirror,
broken crown.

grimm's girls are the princesses with knotted hair
and porcelain for hands,
lips sewn shut with golden thread
and poisonous flowers tucked into their shoes.

grimm's girls are the mermaids,
heads hung backwards
and mouths spilling swamps,
blood streaming sea salt and songs like the sound
of strong men drowning.

grimm's girls are not afraid.
like stars, they know of walking in the dark.
like mother eve, they know of eating the fruit.

LEGACY

i want to be remembered like this:
the girl who was waiting for the beginning of the world,
the last empty seat on the bus,
the extra five minutes of sleep you got this morning,
the one flower that refused to die
when winter came.

the bus ticket when
you needed one,
the dream you never woke up from,
the book you were reading when you
got the best news of your life,
the day that made you
believe in magic.

i want to be remembered like this:
standing in a storm of dreams with my hands open,
saying,
it's okay.
fall.

RABBIT HOLES

i'm sorry for the things i said when
the moon was full.

it's funny,
the people and places and moments we call forever
and then never see again.

in the place where you left me,
the blood is still warm.
the faucet is still running.

there are words for this,
i know them.
i used to be filled with them.

i could not be the graveyard dirt
you used to bury
your dreams.

in the place where you left me,
the engine is still going,
the sparrows won't sing.

so strange,
falling in love with wolves,
then leaving because of the teeth.

YOU

i do not take pride in saying
that i would have stayed forever.

i do not take pride in saying
that i would have you back even now.

every poem like this
is another trauma,
throwing myself in front of the bus.

"it's so good that you're writing again."

i mean,
it is.

i mean,
to know how to save me,
it's got to kill me first.

FOR THE PERSON MY BROTHER WILL MARRY

he is so good.

i do not say this because he is my blood and bone
or because he was the only plant that ever
grew in my hands.

he is just good.

the sort of good that doesn't have an addendum
the sort of good that makes watching the news easier.
the sort of good that carries others.

with him and for him,
i have survived the bombs.
with him and for him,
i have woken up for another fight.

i do not just give you my brother.
i give you my reason.

i have watched him grow from smile to soul to boy to
man,
but in my heart we are still children making tents out of
shadows,
we are still the casualties of being,
we are still strung together like tin cans.
we are still the sounds that drowned out the screaming.

and still, he is good.

LETTERS TO THE PEOPLE WHO HAVE DISSAPOINTED ME

i. i am wearing a crown of thorns
plucked from the stem of your rose;
all the strength you admired in me
was earned from surviving your lows.

ii. god, how could you look at the big bang
for its breaking,
and not a universe
in the making?

iii. i have long been a cathedral for your sins,
knowing so little of staying,
knowing so much about letting in.

iv. but i won't offend my demons
by giving them your name,
the parts of me that you sewed scarlet
and made me wear as shame.

v. and thank you,
thank you,
thank you
for these little deaths,
so often worth the fight.

for the bravest thing
i've ever done
is live my life
despite.

PERSEPHONE AND EURYDICE

in every version of the myth,
it is so much braver to be orpheus,
who played his lyre,
who cried,
who fell into the depths of hell
for his eurydice.

she earns no story
aside from what his sorrow allows.
more muse than maiden,
more brushstroke than paint.

she is only she
when he is sad about it.

i'd like to think that eurydice
was more than just a skeleton
of bristles and bones.
that she was a writer,
that she snored when she slept,
that her hands were unscarred
when orpheus claimed her out of hell.

because she never tried to climb out of it.

(that persephone was gentle
when she touched her on the soul.)

"you are more than just muse.
you are more than what he cares to know."

when you think orpheus,
you think mistake,
heartbreak,
the chance he didn't take.

when i think eurydice,
i think the queen of the underworld
and the duchess of myth.
ghost eyes on pale skin,
bent flower stems, wide hips.

how heavenly it was,
her hell,
how it kissed her on the lips.

WHEN I THINK AUTUMN, I THINK THE FALL

when you think autumn,
you think change.
i think slitting my throat
with the knives in your mouth.

i think last year, this time,
we were still together.
i think lips bleeding berries,
i think hillsides like the beginning and end of the world.

you think rain.
i think fire,
i think drought,
i think of the cores rotting inside
of the apples we picked,
i think of the harvest moon fading,
short skirts, tongue quick.

when you think autumn,
you think the leaves.
rewind the tapes,
it looks like you're falling from the trees.

i think,
and you leave.

LOVE AFFAIR WITH A VAMPIRE

let's address the elephant in the room.
he did not sparkle,
but he was so damn cold.
in his presence,
i'd open the refrigerator for warmth.

no bloodshed,
but he left bruises on my neck
and drained the dreams out of me.
words as sharp as teeth,
hanging upside down and begging me
to see things his way.

sleepless nights,
amusement in my frights,
couldn't meet his own eyes in the mirror,
couldn't kiss me beneath the sun.

the count of my end,
he wanted to turn me into something
dead like him,
feeding off everything
that grew in me.

frankenstein,
meet your monster;
love doesn't live here,
just its impostor.

i've come to slay
the man who stole my life.

here's a lesson that the books
never taught you:
once you kill a girl,
nothing can ever kill her again.

IN THE BATHROOM STALL OF A RESTSTOP ALONG A ROUTE SOMEWHERE IN PENNSYLVANIA WHERE YOU CAN SEE EVERY DAMN STAR

i wrote,
dear andromeda,

i am finally
unchained.

THE REST

no one ever knows me quite as well
as they think they do.

there are secrets i keep even from myself.
there are things that i whisper even when i am
the only person in the room.

i stand before the mirror,
but the girl on the other side
is just a sister
twice removed.

she smiles,
i flinch.

she bends,
and i break.

when you are an artist,
even your reflection
is an invention.

sometimes i must turn the lights off
so that i can truly see myself.

ADVICE

i. the human heart is a halloween party, my darling.
so many things will come knocking at your door,
dressed up like love.

ii. you are not missing
anything you chose to give.

iii. you are not missing
anything they took from you either.

iv. stop excusing people for the things
that which you can't even forgive yourself.

v. first, the prince will do anything for you,
then only some things,
then barely anything.
when the story ends,
make sure that you and the witch remain friends.

vi. you cannot write yourself out of this place;
you have your legs for that.

vii. love is beekeeping:
take the honey and the sting with the same hands.

viii. you are jealous of what's golden,
but you're afraid to let the light in.

ix. let the light in.

ARTHUR

no one ever talks about the stone
that arthur pulled the sword out of.

what happened to it after,
so robbed of its purpose,
regarded only for holding his legacy in.

from ages fourteen to twenty,
i started every sentence with
i don't want to be THAT GIRL but…
look, i hate to be THAT GIRL, i just…

because THAT GIRL is crazy,
THAT GIRL never sleeps,
THAT GIRL doesn't flinch at the sight of blood,
THAT GIRL is rage,
THAT GIRL is unstable,
THAT GIRL screams
and wants to know what heard her,
THAT GIRL seeps into everything like a stain.

but THAT GIRL did not plant herself here
just so that you could grow out of her.
THAT GIRL did not open herself up
to give you more room.

THAT GIRL wants to be all bones and teeth
and hair and crowns.
THAT GIRL wants to be the kind of thing
that makes death want to live.

THAT GIRL wants to die young

and linger forever.

THAT GIRL is the stone,
THAT GIRL is the sword,
THAT GIRL is arthur.

NOTHING WAS FAIR ABOUT VERONA

let's kill ourselves first
and misunderstand each other later.

imagine a love like that:
where we could pluck up dead roses
and watch them come back to life.

we could spit up the poison,
climb down the balcony,
clean up the blood.

i would rather love you as a stranger
than mourn you as a ghost.

ROSALINE

i. you do not realize that
you aren't juliet
until juliet enters act one.

at the climax of your story,
you are just his prologue,
preamble,
preparing the clay for another's hands.

ii. when you were eight years old,
he used to break your dolls in half.
(things were uncomplicated then;
you weren't allowed to play with swords.)

he said,
"have it your way, rosaline.
see? like this.
someday girls will be dying
to be with me."

iii. you never loved him,
you claim.
you are just tired
of being a backstory.
we are all just tired
of being backstories.

iv. during the processions,
you sat by the window and watched.
once they were in the ground,
it rained,

the blood was washed away,
and you could not see where one house ended and the
other began.

your mother was a cold woman.
her hand on your shoulder was gone before it got there.
"that could have been you," she said.

v. you still don't know if this makes you lucky
or not.

GATSBY'S GIRLS

fitzgerald wrote us this way:
with our eyes dead,
our smiles pearl,
our hearts fool's gold.

we poolside ghosts
who never graduated from that one hot summer,
new york city forever on fire
in the distance,
views from behind the champagne glass rim,
sun hats ripped at the brim.

broken perfume bottles,
satin trailing over sewage,
kitchen knives carving diamonds
into some kind of supper.

the newsboys and their headlines:
THE BOYS AND GIRLS ARE KISSING,
THE BOYS AND GIRLS ARE DYING.

we resurrect from the ballrooms,
we still choose excess over bone.

your green light means go;
it's calling us home.

DIVORCE

dear mom and dad,
both of you have asked me
about time travel, fleeting conversations
in the car about
which moment in history i'd go back to,
which disaster i'd stop,
which lips i wouldn't kiss,
which war i would end.

i always laugh and turn to the window,
whisper,
i wouldn't change a thing.

my personal philosophy is that everything
happens for a reason, that every bone broken
is already one on the mend,
that the world is always exactly where it needs to be,
spinning whichever way it needs to spin.

i'm sorry for lying.
at age sixteen, i promised i wouldn't ever again,
but while you change the song on the radio
and take the next left,
i am already fifteen years behind you.

the food is ready, and my school uniform
is drying, the air smells like mowed grass,
febreze, and both of you.
my brother hasn't been born yet,
he's just some north star in the distance,
promising everything and nothing at all.

today is a good day.
the sun is just setting,
mom puts down her sword,
and dad takes off his armor.
we fold our hands together and unbreak our hearts.

we dine in half-silence, half-memory,
and i collect bits and pieces of what you both are
to eat for dessert.

after,
elvis takes pity and sings to your terrible dancing,
i laugh and my heart swells as i watch you,
already forgetting what i never thought
would be so hard to remember.

the future is just folklore,
we are here and now,
a triad of thieves and lovers and fools,
i fall in love with you two first,
the rest of the world later,
the beginning and end of my being.

you kiss me on the forehead
and clear off my plate.
one day,
we will break more than just bread.

dear mom and dad,
here's your answer:
i would just sit down to dinner.
because you don't feel what you're feeling
until you never feel that way again.

DATING PROFILE

someone who will remember
the second packet of sugar.

someone who picks the rose for its thorns,
not despite them.

someone who will stay the whole night
in this haunted house.

someone who could rule a kingdom
with a paper crown.

someone who will feed the ghosts
until they are no longer hungry for this skin.

someone who will touch me into
the next creation myth.

someone who will see the midnight in me
and still want to stay up late.

someone.

NAISSANCE

"have you ever been in love?"

"yes."

"what did it feel like?"

i think of you,
i think of one night feeling like one thousand.
i think of us with our claws out,
trying to hold hands,
wolves among the apple trees,
mistaking everything for blood.

i think of the fact that i started this poem
three years ago
about somebody else.

i do not know if this makes me romantic or not:

until you,
i couldn't finish it.

MAP OF THE IMAGINATION

uncharted, mostly.
the smell of smoke, cherries,
crushed roses, and candle wax upon entry.
the feeling of being kissed, but that is the oxygen here.

the roads are heart vessels,
the sidewalks are bleeding,
the blood here is candy,
the candy is bittersweet.

somewhere inside,
i have made it out of reality
alive.

SPLIT ME IN HALF

from my chest will pour

one dozen roses / the feather from the back of a black
sparrow / a map of my own world / letters i have not
yet sent / my father's wrath / my mother's fury / a
tangle of pearl and gold / one broken perfume bottle /
all the words of those who left / the river from which i
first drank the earth

GODDESSES LOVE GODDESSES

you fall in love with her,
and it kills you.
but you still visit the temples,
you still sacrifice your skin.

persephone wants the garden of your body –
every winter massacres the roses,
every spring massacres you.

medusa just wants you
to look her in the eye,
and it's a kind of suicide
when you believe that
it'll be different this time.

aphrodite wants you by the window
with your shirt off, mouthful of poetry
that gets lost in translation
on the way to her tongue.

athena wants you holy and golden
on the floor of the woods,
making love to the sound of the
war in your mind.

you fall in love with her, and it kills you.
on your knees,
hands folded in prayer,
legs spread in sin.

when the gods open you up,
let the right one in.

AUTUMN SONGS

here is the part you thought you'd never get to.
honeysuckles, the moon, not surviving – being. smiling
at your reflection, swimming in leaves, lips spilling cider
on your way along the trees. fresh dirt: dying and
burning and ripening earth. thread caught in your
spread fingers and a scar healing up your spine, mind
spun in a corn maze, back bent over a pumpkin patch.
dirt: hard, breathing, growing, just like your bones. a
chill in the air, calloused hands clutching the necklace at
your chest, barnyards, crickets, fools in love in leather
in lace dancing in the dark. kissing in the dark. laying
thistles and bread at the grave of the person you
decided not to be.

here comes the after. here comes the epilogue. here is
the part you thought you'd never get to. you're alive.

ANYTHING, EVERYTHING

do you want to bleed?
we can bleed.

do you need me to be merciless?
i'll be merciless.

i'd move to the forest,
i'd bend my back over the trees.

make a deal with the witch,
defeat the witch,
become the witch.

i'd take the apple,
the pomegranate,
open up my chest without a key.

i'd walk into the sun
and turn my back to the moon.

i'd do anything you wanted me to.
but you don't want that,
do you?

WHAT DO YOU WANT ME TO DO TO YOU?

baby,
i am an old kitchen in a modern home,
it is sunday dinner and
inside of me,
i want you to come and feast.

i am an excavation site,
the want inside of me is ancient,
dig up the sound in my throat
that i've been searching for
and brush off the past with your fingertips.

i am a mountain that
many think they can move.

please,
erupt something in me.

THREE, TWO, ONE...

the new year came
like the sort of unwanted guest
you grow fond of.

the oddest things turned me nostalgic:
dead christmas trees by the sewer,
listening to auld lang syne on the car radio,
hearing the muffled countdown through the hall door.

i guess i'm just trying to say that growing up
doesn't mean forgetting you.
it means saying, "look, that happened"
and taking the lights down until next year.

AFTER

at the hair salon,
the woman asks what she can do for me today,
and i tell her that i want to look like a girl
you would never have fallen in love with.

i want to look like a girl who doesn't do
the things i used to do.

i want to build a life without the bricks of you.

MAPS

here are the bones,
here is the wreckage that we called home.

here is an unfortunate lie:
in time, i could have loved you better.

but i am not a thing that loves or
can be loved.

i am selfish.
i planted the seeds of adventure in you
to take you out for a spin.

here is an unfortunate truth:
i loved the engine more than i loved you.
i miss the mountains more than i miss you.

MILLENNIAL

we are a diaspora
of believers.
we ride in like horsemen of the elements,
a carousel of raining blood
and magnanimous death.

they mock us because
they fear us.

what are we?
chasers of dreams?
the children that time forgot?

we are the lost generation,
too full of empty.

floating in space,
feral and
desperate to make contact.

we scold blasphemy
until we are called god.

YOU SHOULD REALLY PUT YOURSELF OUT THERE

here i am, unfolded.

here i am,
sitting down to dinner
with all this fear.

here i am, cupped palms
waiting for the next hurt.

here i am,
with my hand on the holster
of memory's gun.

here i am,
starting over.

here i am,
homesick for heartbreak.

A LOVE LETTER TO THOSE WHO LOOKED MY EATING DISORDER IN THE EYE BEFORE I COULD

did you say malnourished?
i think i heard milestone.

the worry in your voice
sounded as sharp as applause;
another victory dinner that
i couldn't eat.

of course we became friends.
like me, anorexia was always hungry.
like me, she had teeth.

i was a blind woman
reading the braille of my spine,
my rib cage,
my collar bones,
like some kind of truth.

but i want you to know that i got better,
took down the funhouse mirror,
took up more space in the room.

i want you to know that my mind
is a safe place to live now,
that my hair isn't the only thing that has body,
that these bones which once were a prison
are now called home.

that i have never been prouder
to be bad at math;

no altar at the scale,
no caloric algebra to count out on skeleton bones.

i want you to know that i am no longer
the coldest thing in the room.

i am both the gardener
and the rose.

i am in bloom.

IN THE REALM OF FAIRIES

dear mother,
i'm sorry that i never came home for dinner;
my belly was already full.

dear mother,
you always told me that i would become
something awful if i ate the fruit.

but now i think the point
of the story is that if you chose to eat the fruit,
you were already something awful.

dear mother,
i want to be the kind of thing
that the darkness fears.
when i laugh,
i want black magic to spill out of my mouth
like blood.

from their backs
spring bat wings,
from their hands,
poison berries come to harvest.

the night court swims
in a river of limbs,
teeth,
and red wine.

dear mother,
in it,
i open my mouth

and pick the fairytales out of my teeth.

dear mother,
i ate the fruit.

sincerely yours,
something awful.

THE JUNGLE BOOK

it's dangerous to raise your kids in the city.
we become concrete, callous things.
howling at the fluorescence because
it's the closest thing we'll get to starlight.

so starved for daylight that we'll
call anything pure.

we scream at the skyline
like iron beasts,
climb up
lamppost moons.

born from leather,
skin like concrete,
we are always just waking up,
always waiting for the train,
always wiping away that big apple blood.

finding bruises
from nights that we can't remember.
here,
summer still looks like december.

ahead of time
and losing our minds,

there is a restlessness that we were born with:
never lose,
never sleep,
never die.

it is a terrifying thing,
to live where everyone else wants to be,
at the end of the world,
nowhere left to run,
nothing more to see.

MYTHOLUTION

and what of the persephone you used to be?
what of the peonies that
once stemmed from the soil of your youth?

what of the hera you are now?
snapping his lightening bolt in half,
using the pieces to stir your tea.

what if both were
a fine thing to be?

CONTINENTAL AFFAIR

they say that the best way to get over someone
is to get under someone else.
so when they leave you,
leave, too.

relearn touch through the plane ticket's paper cut,
press your fingers into the earth and leave it quaking,
a seismic connection,
tracking the beat of your heart until it's
category eight,
leaving dead memories in its wake.

ride the road
and let it wear a different face as you go;
the bartender,
the museum guard,
caricatures on the plaza,
the motel owner's daughter.

wear your nicest dress and let
the mountains wine and dine you,
one million miles behind you
down an aisle marked route 66.

wrap the atlas around your naked skin,
candlelight in the valley
while you dine in sin.

squint your eyes until you can't tell
the difference between lip prints and passport stamps,
lost in love,
infatuated with the journey.

look away from the phone and up at the sky.
the moon will be there despite the phase it's in, darling.

it's what you need.
it only knows how to come back.
it doesn't lie.

HOW TO HEAL

one. there was a time with them that made you cry, made you avoid your own eyes in the mirror, made you think of always and expiration dates. the book they never read, the poem they laughed at, the necklace blaring the wrong birthstone.

put it in someplace obvious, someplace that'll show its teeth when it smiles. a reminder. this is the only time you're allowed to be unkind to yourself.

two. do not torture yourself with fantasies of apologies and possibilities, nor sweet serendipities. live everyday certain that it is not them at the door or on the phone or back to you at the coffee shop. live everyday sure that you will never see them again, even if it feels like one million little deaths.

because the chance of them will not heal you. find closure in the growth of your own bones.

three. it will be tempting, but do not look. i promise that you do not want to know.

four. go to the place you once thought could only be beautiful beside them. stand there and cry if you need to. but open your eyes long enough to look at how it went on, existing. that is a lesson, not a tragedy.

do not let them become the paint on the walls.

five. listen to the song you first slow danced to – firebugs, flushed cheeks, pink lips – listen to it and sing it hard and ugly. salt, wound, salt, wound. scream it off your rooftop, again and again until the lyrics are more you than you are them.

it's your song now.

six. go to the place, listen to the song, do not look. wash, rinse, and repeat.

seven. one day, you will wake up and think of the mozzarella sticks you'll have for lunch or the reality television show you fell asleep watching last night, and then it'll make you sob, that random thought you had.

because, for the first time in forever, it wasn't them.

eight. clear the nightstand, remove the bandage. you do not need to be unkind. you do not need the reminder.

A MEMORY

he laughs,
"shakespeare was not a romantic,"
and shuts the book in my face.

but have i loved any differently?

the rashness,
the knives,
the blood.

SEVEN LETTERS TO LUCIFER FROM GOD

i. morning star,
king of babylon,
what is it that you call yourself now?

ii. perhaps i loved you too softly,
perhaps i should have kissed
more fear onto your tongue.

peter will read this.
i digress.

iii. by the time i warned you not to play with matches,
you were already on fire.
by the time i tried to knight you,
you were already wearing a crown.

morning star,
when i called you my lion heart,
did you not take it as a compliment?
when i gave you your wings,
did you mistake a gift for an opportunity?

iv. they say that you can only love a king for so long
before you must become one yourself.

how terrible,
that your idea of heaven
could be someone else's hell.

v. i keep writing prayers through the lips
of dying men in case you might hear them.
as we forgive those who

---

trespass against us.

i keep spitting out meteors
to understand what you felt,
but they barely break the earth.

vi. morning star,
don't tell the angels
that i would trade them all
even
for this singed version of you.

vii. once, we were out smoking on a cloud,
you leaned over and
lit my cigarette with your halo.

i warned,
"careful,
you might fall."

CLUE, FOR THE BROKEN-HEARTED

in our family home,
with your suitcase packed.

at the bottom of the wine glass,
with my childhood on the line.

under the desk,
with my leg shaking beneath your hand.

in the back stairwell,
with my heart between my legs.

at prom,
with a drink.

after i wrote my first book,
with my words lost on you.

right here, right now,
with my life in your hands.

and you?
playing catch.

DUAL

i ran after myself,
but i could not keep up.
i ran from myself,
but she's the one who knows me best.
i ran into myself,
i keep running into myself.

this is a lifetime of setting out clothes
for whichever girl i will wake up as in the morning.

the only way i can describe it:
one minute the beast is chasing me.
the next minute,
i am the beast.

IT WAS JUST LOCKER ROOM TALK

if boys will be boys,
then girls must be wolves.

if they are down by the reservoir,
killing each other with toy guns,
we must be one thousand ophelias
floating upriver like the dead come alive.

the undercurrent of the man's tale,
knife in hand looking for hamlet, shouting,
i would rather be a fish without a bicycle
than a book without a spine.

if they are in the locker room, then we must descend
from the posters with our claws out and teeth sharp,
curl out from under their tongues and cut them off,
unbend from under their feet,

take back our skin,
take back the streets.

if boys will be boys,
these girls won't be sweet.

THE GIRLS YOU MEET IN STORIES

i. the girl before the wolf, the whimper behind the howl, the puddle of daylight melting before the full yellow moon. dresses threaded with slivers of amber fur, bared porcelain teeth, and claws painted the color that used to remind her of home. the boy leaving breadcrumbs for those eyes in the woods.

nothing to be afraid of. just a girl i used to know.

ii. a marionette girl in love with her handler – made of oak, string, and curiosity. she loved those hands, those callouses, those heart lines, from the moment they crafted her out of bone and air. gave her eyes, gave her joints, painted her lips in a permanent smile. strings bound to every finger like engagement rings, he took her dancing across stages, made her move, made her feel alive.

but who knew that love could be a hobby? or that he owned scissors so sharp?

who knew that she was just a piece of wood to a man who had more?

iii. a sea-born antoinette, a pile of damp tendrils interwoven with shells and seaweed, a shipwreck of a girl with a toothy grin and rolling country; white, drenched dresses and ruffles made of eels. stilts on waves, high on high waters, there is nothing more excessive than a kingdom in the deep.

she shouts, "then let them taste the sea."

iv. a wired-up eve, a biblical myth just out of time. adam with metal bones and a glitch in his lies, her with hair dripping silver and a code of him inside of her. the trees are electric, the sins just as much. the snake rattles its tongue everyday at 8pm and the sky switches off on cue.

"there is no part of you that isn't me," adam says to her, a warning, glowing blue and loving red.

her finger sparks and the world crackles when she breaks the chip where a rib should be – sets the ground aflame. "now, there is no part of you."

v. suburbia, the girl. dead moss eyes, cut knees under white pleated skirts, voice sickly sweet like a cicada song, nice and numbing. her skin is made of honeydew and heartbreak, out behind the quick mart – baby food, beer, and doll dresses with dirt on the hem.

she's got wandering eyes and pencil shavings on her mary janes, grass cuts tattooed to the backs of her legs, a copy of good housekeeping bloodied on her windowsill. but if you ask her about it, she'll just smile.

nothing happens here.

vi. an artist's muse, eyes in watercolor, lips in acrylic, one brush handle spine and her backbone like an easel. he gives her the pearl girl's brood and mona lisa's smile, gives her one-one hundredth of every woman he's ever seen.

she licks the color off his left cheek and smiles against the wall, "paint me like one of your real girls; bring me to life with the tremble of my canvas skin."

DREAM, DREAM, DREAM

i've got your hands
in my hands,
all of our problems in the kitchen sink.

you bend into me,
and i call you armstrong,
laying down your discovery,
one calloused finger across everyone of my
moonbeams.

before you,
love was store-brand,
princess-cut,
hallmark,
half-smiles,
"we don't have much in common
but thank god a first date finally went well."

after you,
love was freckle-shaped,
michelangelo's mistake,
the gas station god couldn't touch,
always past midnight,
always with our hands open,
always bones
and mortar
and paper cuts.

i thought i knew this by heart,
afraid to write another love poem
that would leave me shaking the stanzas off my skin.

but here i am,
at dawn,
at birth,
at the beginning.

edison,
this love is electric.
you've invented something in me.

INAUGURATION DAY

in my dream,
snow white wakes up,
unclenches her fist,
and tells the prince that she doesn't want to be kissed.

she demands to be known by the fire
raging inside of her,
but she is porcelain, and they name her so.

the more breakable we are,
the more beautiful we become.

in my dream,
i choose to be hideous.
i open my mouth and from it spills
a tangle of thorns,
a wolf choking on the full moon,
heat and blood and angles.

in my dream,
they burn my sisters and i at the stake
for having the tongues of witches
and we smile when we complain about the chill.

we build our homes
on the pavement,
the front of the bus,
the edge of the nile,
the bottom of the vial,
hug ourselves to feel the earth.

in my dream,
we do not rewrite history;
when they bend us over,
we reach for the future.

on our knees,
we gather the soil from which
our daughters will grow.

in my dream,
we are dorothy,
we are the wicked witches.
we keep our knives ruby red and sharpened,
aimed at the man behind curtain,
and march forth.

the wizard will see us now.

AS I AM

i saw a train wreck once
and didn't even react to it.

i was an addict,
fresh off my dose of ruination,
already in the home of the third victim's wife,
collecting the pearls off her floor,
reading the note he wrote for her
on a receipt before he left for work that morning.

last year,
the boy said i am breaking up with you
and i cried
not for him but for all the fights we had not yet had,
all the teeth we hadn't yet shown.

i told him this and he said,
you know, you're really fucked up.

i want to blame it all on my parents,
all that i breathed in during
the breaks from their chokeholds.
i want to blame it on the dog that hates its collar
but doesn't know what to do without it on.

i want to blame it on my absence,
the only thing about me that ever shows up,
and how i kept asking you to open the closet door
but you kept opening the bedroom door.

we were speaking in dialogues
from two different books,

tragedy and comedy,
the latter somehow the more depressing,
pasted sloppily together line by line,
ransom notes for chapters,
taking all of this just for something in return.

i want to blame it on the things i saw when i was little
that kids ought not to see,
the adultery i read as children's books.
and the roses that kept growing even when
we stopped watering the garden.

i want to blame it on how
you kept calling me a train wreck,
and i just kept saying thank you.

SOMETHING WICKED

we are not the witches you are afraid of.
we are worse.

we were birds in flight,
so you gave us beaked noses.
you were envious of our magic,
so you saw us in green.

you believed we rode in on
the brooms we used to clean up your mess,
so afraid of enchantment
that you burned us to the bone.

but we do not flock from the west,
we burst from the earth,
midsummer queens,
starflowers bending towards the moon.

incantations murmured into coffee cups,
one eye, two eyes, a third eye,
handkerchiefs unfolding into spell books,
hair cloaking us like weeping willows,
dressed like the wings on crows,
silver rings stacked heavy on skin,
dancing until we are without feet.

we are not the witches you are afraid of.
but you should be.

WHEN POETRY DOESN'T WORK

okay,
so you're sitting there with your sad eyes
and your cigarette
on the corner of typical,
putting four walls up around rock bottom
because the one who just broke your heart
knocked fifty points off your credit score,
so who the hell is going to rent their chest out
to you now?

you don't wash your hair,
just turn on the television and look for the channel
where they're playing
the night you got drunk and danced on the bed
and said
"you're like the shard of glass
i never wanted in my heart,
but now i'll die if you ever take it out."

i get it.

here's your permission.
sometimes you have to wait and see how bad it gets
before you can understand how bad it's getting.
sometimes you have to throw yourself to the wolves
just to see if there's anything there to save.
sometimes you have to become your worst nightmare
to know what your worst nightmare is.

love doesn't live here tonight.
allow yourself this day of the dead
and live inside of the skin you tried to throw away.

prick your finger on the spindle,
try to find a metaphor in the church
that just exploded in north dakota,
and kiss the wrong people with your tongue.

for me, healing is never a decision.
i offer my bones to recovery until it spits them all out
saying, "i need blood."

hope doesn't live here tonight,
and that's okay, it's going to stop by in the morning.
for now, play the titanic just to point out that jack
could have really fit on that mirror,
that perhaps there's no heart inside of a shipwreck,
that sometimes tragedy is just living
inside of more tragedy
and baby, that's all there is.

stop pouring out of yourself with abandon
just to keep the glass half full for everyone else
and call it a night.

allow yourself to feel this.

sometimes children need to touch the stove
and sit with the burn
before realizing
that they never want to feel this way again.

HONESTLY

my entire life has become about trying not to be
the girl you turned me into;
in doing that,
i am still exactly the girl you turned me into.

i guess that all i'm trying to say
is that if the only power i have
is in seeking power over you,
then i am powerless after all.

you spread my legs
without using your hands,
and i already feel like a piece
of lint that you're going to flick off
your coat later.

i am ash on a cigarette,
i am snow on a summer's day,
i am the eyelash you wish on
before you forget it forever.

why am i so good at being yours
when it took me a decade
to become my own?

SO YOU WANT TO KNOW HOW I'VE BEEN DOING?

dear journal,
i've been doing a lot of messed up things
to find the poetry lately.

they call this hill "damage point."
past it, you can see the hands of hades,
over it, you can see the stars.

i kissed two strangers last night
like a succubus stealing pain
for my art.

when they bit back,
i used the blood to write it all down.

look, i'm fine,
there are a few more TURN BACK signs
up ahead.

look,
i said i'm fine.
that's the problem.

dear journal,
i'm so proud of who i am,
but i'm not proud of what i'm proud of.

THE OTHER WOMAN

i look into his eyes,
and you blink back at me.
you put your hand over his heart
and it echoes the way i say his name.

in this tug of war,
our arms are tired,
and he is sipping a
piña colada.

he kisses your lipstick
onto my lips,
and i realize that
we wear the same shade:
original sin.

we have so much in common;
i wonder if secretly we are
in love with each other
through the vessel of him.

AFTER HAPPILY EVER AFTER

i wish there was a support group
for happy people
who once weren't.

what do i do with all of this peace?
where do i drive off the road to recovery?

i wish there was a support group
for people who no longer accept the things
they used to.

post-chaos 101:
coping with being able to cope.

what do i pack in my bag in place
of the bones
and the razor blades?

how do you live in a foreign body?
how do you smile back at a reflection you don't
recognize?

the ascension,
the struggle,
the climb
has been who i am for so long
that i have no idea what to do at the top of the
mountain.

the whole world is at my feet,
but i'm itching to cut my leg open
back on the trail.

everyday it rained in the village.
when the gods gave it some sun,
the people just wanted to know what
would happen to all of the crops they grew
just to make do.

SOLITUDE, OR FALLING IN LOVE WITH YOURSELF

it happened all at once,
this shift in the midst
of my sadness,
the frustration of picking up the phone
with no one left to call.

slowly i realized that even when i was alone,
i had always had company.
so i began to take myself out for coffee.

for walks,
for journeys,
for dates,
to the library,
to the movies,
to other countries.

those thoughts,
that voice in my head
which had once been a burden –
i began to listen.

i turned off the sad girl songs
and pulled out the wedding track list
i had been holding onto for the great "someday"
and slow danced wholly with myself.

got strong enough
to hold me in my own arms.

stopped asking what others saw in me
and began looking
to see what i could find within myself,
woman of my own dreams.

for this person with my same skin,
she is all that i have.
she has been there for me even
when i've turned on her,
had the nerve to hold a knife to her throat,
wanting to end her life without conscience.

so when the world made her feel unclean,
i bathed her.
for all the things she had done,
i showed the empathy that i gave out
like christmas to others,
and i forgave her.

silly.

i had long been looking
for a friend
but never bothered to ask
the girl living inside of my body.

last night,
i put down the phone
and gave her a call.

HOW TO LOSE HER

let her pour her heart out
without raising your glass,

remind her with every missed call
that girls in love finish last.

tell her who you are,
then shed your snakeskin come fall.

promise her everything,
then break the pinky off.

lure her in with love,
then leave her on the hook.

say she shines so brightly it hurts your eyes,
so you don't even bother to look.

turn the purity of her love
into a dirty game you like to play.

win her over as one man,
and then, like a magician!
suddenly change.

see her learn herself
through all she bore
and what remains.

congratulations,
she knows her worth.
now watch her walk away.

CUSP

when i leave a place,
i see it for the first time.

i say goodbye to everyone with my hands open,
grabbing all the things they couldn't give me
in their presence.

i eat the loss,
i dig through the absence.

this does not make me an optimist
or even an opportunist.

i'm afraid that i am this way.
i'm afraid that in death,
i will still be wanting.

KISMET

we are always out of time, aren't we?
always out of patience,
always out of our minds,
always calling each other's names from opposite stars,
waiting for gravity to catch up with fate.

shifting the letters around in the word "almost"
until they look like the walls
of a home.

we are fast cars,
comets,
parallel lines,
but i would rather collide and die
than spend a lifetime of passing you by.

THE WOMEN

i saw one dozen roses crushed to death
on the pavement today,
and i wondered what love story
chose to end at 4pm on a sunday afternoon.

i took this street because i was running late
after talking to the barista at the coffee shop
who told me that her mother
liked her coffee the way i drank it,
but there was no fondness there.

that morning,
she'd gotten off the phone with the woman
who birthed her and took five long breaths
before she could prepare herself to continue
being alive, cracked open frankenstein,
desperate to figure out if monster makes man
or if man makes monster.

it came up in book club last week,
but just for a second because
this girl named amber couldn't stop going on and on
about her new haircut, even though everyone knew
she'd only gotten it to mask that terrible dye job
from the week before.

and look,
marie of marie's hair salon on third
is usually much better at what she does;
she's got a four point three-star rating on yelp
thank you very much, but lately,
she's just been worried about her little sister.

she's been seeing this guy
who's married but *oh my god, marie*
he swears he's going to leave her soon.

marie's sister?
her name is felicity,
and her hair is like the sun.

every time she kisses him, it's like a ménage a trois;
so much of his wife still on his tongue,
so much of herself to keep the house haunted.

so today she gives him an ultimatum,
leave her, be with me, *be with me,*
because its easier to break the heart of a photograph
than your own.

but he can't,
so she won't,
and the story ends with a bouquet at her heel
and a slap across his face so sharp
it whips him back home in time to catch his wife
coming through the door.

i set the groceries on the counter,
give him a kiss,
ask, "did you see all those dead flowers outside?"

OLDER

i am finally the girl
i wrote about becoming
in my diary when i was thirteen years old.

the views are great here,
i just didn't expect it to be so cold.

i am always cutting myself open,
delivering myself to the next dream.

i am a matryoshka doll,
always nesting.

always waiting for the day
there isn't anymore
to pull out from inside of me.

PERSPECTIVE

when i was younger,
there was a creature that lived
underneath my bed,
scratched at the hardwood,
growled in its slumber,
eyes yellow and
fur creeping
while i was sleeping.
sometimes,
i was afraid.
other times,
it would sing me songs
in a language i didn't know,
speak of a world floors deep
where the darkness kept its vacation home.
we became friends,
the bond of solitude,
the company of alone.
i only saw its face once when
i was twenty-five
and visiting my childhood home.
i called after it,
"monster under my bed!"
this would be the first and only time,
a flash of fur that went to hide.
it blinked at me and said,
"you have always been
the monster under mine."

PRINCESS

zeus sleeps,
atlas sits,
persephone plucks the last rose.

there are chapters of this story
that we don't read.
there are verses of this song,
lips pressed together,
that we don't sing.

i've forgotten how to forget you,
but in this land of lies,
you are what's true.

i was the tide,
and you were the moon.
you were waiting to breathe,
and i was waiting for you.

SIGN OF THE CROSS

i grew up in catholic school;
i'm convinced that was my downfall.

i am always kneeling at the altar,
mistaking love for religion.

sacrifice,
in the beginning,
open cuts,
cathedral yells,
on my knees,
mortal sin,
finger to my bottom lip,
do not covet thy neighbor's wife,
eat the fruit,
do not eat the fruit,
what about thy neighbor?

the bible is a five-letter word for
loopholes and terrible vision,

saw your red flags as red roses,
every sign telling me to run,
but never specifying in which direction.

love is a kind of haunting,
allowing ourselves to be killed
and then choosing to stay.

isn't this how we were taught
to give?

you could cut me open,
and i would be grateful –
calling it holy,
body and blood, blood and body.

you could ruin my life,
and i would still whisper your name in prayer.

you could tear me to pieces,
and i would help you hide the bones.

THE ARTISTIC PROCESS

                    the rose,
                  the dagger,
                   the wand,
                    the pen.

allow me to explain.

(the rose)

i begin with what the earth gives me.
i visit the gardens,
i pray to the flowers,
i take a lesson from them about growing.

i write a bad metaphor
about the sun and the way
it's burning.

i lose myself in the woods,
paper's beginning,
and in return,
the woods find me.

i sit under a storm and soak in
all the pain that the sky must
have been holding.

i stare into the sunset and say,
"beautiful."
and the sunset asks,
"why?"

(the dagger)

next,
i stab myself in the chest
with a picture of my ex.

i call the people who have wronged me.
i allow myself to feel the things
i usually can't look in the eye,
all of the things i kill in myself in order to survive.

i open the book of things i'm not proud of,
pandora, my old friend.
drown in journal entries
written by the girl i no longer am.

i disappear into myself
like a magician's second,
open old wounds,
dig around with dirty hands inside.

i'll apologize later.

right now,
i must hurt
and harvest the blood.

(the wand)

i throw myself into the path of the unreal
and unknown,
give up my body,
ask the trees what they've seen

and what they know.

close my eyes and trip over time,
eat the cake,
drink from the vial,
waltz with the tornado,
step off the windowsill with peter.

grow wings and
dare myself to fly.
dance with the creatures
that own the night.

(the pen)

and then
i sit down.

and then
i write.

SEASON'S GREETINGS

for those who saw broken glass
at the end of october
and thought of the holiday season.

store windows,
cranberry sauce,
kitchen knives.

for those who cannot stomach the holly:
all that green and red,
moss and blood.

for those who thrive on the lights,
swallow them whole
to find warmth in themselves.

for those who need december.
for those who pretend there are eleven months.

for those who celebrate all
or one
or none.

for those waiting on the corner
of heartbreak,
present still wrapped.

for those who seek the pine
only because
it's how they remember the mountains.

whether it was as simple as

a snowfall
or as difficult as a blizzard:
thank you for surviving.

and to all a good night.

JOURNAL ENTRIES

OCTOBER 2, 2015
today was dreadful, and i'm exhausted. it feels as though my bones are breaking over and over again. there are constants: [they] are horrible, my anxiety winds me tight in red string and rope made for hanging. hours wasted with this man's ten faces, bearing the brunt of his boyhood. it's too much, but nothing is enough. i collect promises like sour candy, like dead flower petals, like splintered wood. in the gamble of second chances, i've somehow become a dealer. i don't know if i can go on with this existing.

i'm still sad. i wish i wasn't. i'm *trying*. i hope that someday treats me better than today. if i can make it until then.

OCTOBER 2, 2016
and just like that, it all turned into autumn. i've been doing so much thinking lately. no reinventing; just growing. how much of my misery have i chosen? how much of my hell have i purchased real estate in for the comfort? sitting in therapy today, walking with coffee and potential in my hands, smiling at strangers even in the rain, i felt something mystic, something calm, something wonderful. and the fear that i haven't done enough, been enough, seen enough – that i've been doing it all wrong began to fade.

i am ascended. i am at peace. i am between this world and the next. i choose not to be sad forever. i choose to start page one on page 7,787. i have accepted all of the girls i have been in the same breath that i greet the woman i am becoming. i accept that despite it all, i am still soft, and that is still the strongest thing i can be. i forgive myself for the ruin. today, i begin to build. today, i am free.

GREAT AGAIN

so here is your throne.
here are the prejudices that you call home.
here are the eyes of young girls closing,
legs opening,
patchwork pulled from the seams,
skin pulled from the seams
to hang up as curtains.

so here is what you didn't care about:
new york city, a hand down my pants in the subway
and me, not wanting to upset him.
my grandmother with her back bent over an ancestry,
trying to carry it home.

so here is your future,
a room full of red hats and plastic masks
using skin color as curse words,
using "she" as a symptom,
using hate in a hailstorm as shelter.

turn off the television
and look in the mirror.
there is his throne.

INTO SUMMER

in new york,
it snows one day
and blisters heat the next.

i have the nerve
to convince myself
that i can't change.

THE ADRENALINE JUNKIE

it is not a coincidence
that both in moments of pure ecstasy
and pure terror,
we scream.

my therapist says,
it sounds like you're having a love affair with fear.
how do you feel about that?
i respond,
i guess it scares me.

fear puts a want in me that i cannot describe,
takes me to the movies,
some b-grade horror,
and slashes me to life.

so charming, this fear of mine,
puts its hand on my back by some train tracks,
asks if i want to go for a dive.

fear kisses me awake at night,
sings me to sleep come morning.
it holds my heart still for me on the coasters,
the cliff sides,
by the coffins.

knits the dark into a blanket for me,
wraps the snake around my shoulders like a shawl.

fear has its hands in my hair
and its fingers between my lips,
whispering in my ear

to look death right in the eye.

clasps its hand over my mouth
when i dare say: "too high."
fear knows what gets me going,
electric fences,
glass shards,
haunted homes,
takes me running with scissors around the reservoir,
takes me deep into the woods,
leaves me all alone.

my therapist says,
it sounds like you're out chasing thrills,
how do you feel about that?
i respond,

fear is a fickle lover,
when it clings to me,
i cling back.

but the longer it stays,
the longer it's gone.

HEROES

you say,
"go back in time;
you get to stop the war,
but it means that you never meet me –
what do you do?"

what kind of person
has loving you turned me into?

no matter what i answer,
you don't forgive me.

don't you understand?
love is a selfish, awful thing
that always separates hero from human.

saving you
is saving my world.

MANIC PIXIE DREAM GIRL?

wild
witch.
nightmare
woman.

SAY HIS NAME

when he fell,
was it easy to call him icarus
when you knew he was the sun?

everyone knows sisyphus for his boulder
and atlas for the bend of his shoulders
and not the boys who were boys
before they became kings.

a body built for war,
a heart thrumming for more –
which do you think will leave a legacy?

they lay him down in dirt
and will remember him as charcoal
and the splatter of blood
instead of paint.

a rose for its thorns,
a plant for its prickle,
patroclus for his limbs.

he changed the world
in one million ways,
but all that's left is the story
of how it tried to change him.

CRAIGSLIST'S MISSED CONNECTIONS, PART TWO

right in front of me,
you still had so much hidden away.

i thought you
might be the moon.

I HAVE A STORY FOR YOU

"and then she fell
down
down
down
the rabbit hole,"
my mother read.

(the white hare,
fur skin,
wide eyes,
half-ticking clocks.)

"turn the page," i whispered,
"i want to know what's inside.
i want to know if she makes it out alive."

ACKNOWLEDGEMENTS

A thank you to my family, who understood that writing was never a choice but my destiny.

Another thank you to every single reader I've ever had. For a writer, the purest love is with those who devour your words.

And to those who have broken my heart – thank you for the material.

ABOUT THE AUTHOR

Naiche Lizzette Parker is a writer, witch, and lover of magic living in New York City. She was born with an abundance of words inside of her, and she's hoping to get them down on paper before her time is through.

INSTAGRAM: naichelizzette
TUMBLR: crooked-queen.tumblr.com
TWITTER: naichelizzette
EMAIL: naichelizzetteparker@gmail.com
WEBSITE: naichelizzette.com

Made in the USA
San Bernardino, CA
14 February 2019